HEALTHY HABIT COOKBOOK

Great-tasting recipes lower in fat and calories

INTRODUCTION

Delightfully rich and creamy, Dannon® Yogurt is meant to be enjoyed throughout life. It not only tastes great, but it's one of the healthiest food choices you can make. Whether you enjoy Dannon Yogurt as a snack or part of a meal, you'll benefit from the high levels of calcium, protein and potassium found in each cup. Dannon Yogurt is something the whole family will love. It's ideal for infants, makes a marvelous portable snack for children and teens and is a low-calorie, nutrient-dense choice for adults—all the more reason to add it to the foods you eat everyday.

Cooking with Yogurt

Dannon Yogurt is an appealing and highly nutritious addition to everything from soups and sandwiches to main dish entrées and desserts. Cooking with Dannon Plain Yogurt reduces fat, calories and cholesterol without sacrificing taste. It's perfect for replacing traditional ingredients, such as milk, cream, mayonnaise, sour cream and cream cheese.

In fact, Dannon Yogurt has the fabulous taste and smooth texture you need to make a healthy difference in many of your favorite dishes. This is why Dannon is the one yogurt so many cooks trust for their own recipes. Discover the excitement of cooking with Dannon Yogurt in this wonderful collection of outstanding recipes. Trust Dannon to make cooking healthy . . . just plain delicious

Dannon®.
A Very Healthy Habit.
For Life.™

Helpful Hints

Dannon Yogurt has a delicate gel structure, so gently stir or fold it into other ingredients. To measure yogurt, spoon it into a dry measuring cup and level it off with a straight-edged spatula.

A liquid, called whey, may separate out of yogurt that has been allowed to stand; simply stir it back in before using.

When cooking with yogurt, be sure to keep the heat low. High temperatures can cause separation, evaporation of liquid and a curdled appearance. Flavor and nutrition are not affected.

4. To help prevent yogurt from separating in cooked dishes, combine 1 tablespoon cornstarch and a small amount of yogurt, stir the mixture back into remaining cup of yogurt and use as directed in recipes.

5. To make yogurt cheese: Spoon yogurt into large strainer lined with double thickness of cheesecloth or a coffee filter. Place bowl beneath, but not touching strainer to catch liquid. Cover and chill for 24 hours. Discard liquid.

NUTRITIONAL CHART

	Calories	Fat (g)	Cholesterol (mg)	Calcium (mg)
Dannon® Plain Nonfat Yogurt (1 cup, 8 ounces)	110	0	5	400
Dannon® Plain Lowfat Yogurt (1 cup, 8 ounces)	140	4	15	400
Dannon® Lemon or Vanilla Lowfat Yogurt (1 cup, 8 ounces)	200	3	15	350
Cultured Sour Cream (1 cup)	410	40	85	225
Cream Cheese (8 ounces)	790	79	250	180
Heavy Cream, whipped (1 cup)	830	89	330	155
Mayonnaise (1 cup)	1580	175	130	40
Butter (1 cup)	1630	184	500	50

ENERGIZING BREAKFASTS

Orange French Toast

1 cup fresh orange juice
2 tablespoons grated orange peel
1 tablespoon frozen orange juice
    concentrate, thawed
5 eggs
2 tablespoons granulated sugar
½ cup DANNON® Plain Nonfat or Lowfat
    Yogurt
1 loaf braided bread or brioche bread
1 tablespoon butter or margarine
    Confectioner's sugar
    Orange slices

In a large bowl combine orange juice, orange peel, orange juice concentrate, eggs and granulated sugar. Beat until well blended. Stir in yogurt. Cut bread into 1- to 1½-inch-thick slices (about 16 slices). Dip bread slices into egg mixture, turning to coat. Place in single layer in a shallow pan. Pour any remaining egg mixture over slices. Cover; chill up to 2 hours.

Heat griddle or large skillet over medium-high heat. Melt butter in pan. Lightly brown French toast on both sides. Keep French toast warm in oven until ready to serve. Dust with confectioner's sugar and garnish with orange slices before serving.   *8 servings*

Nutritional information per serving:

500 Calories   9 g Fat   140 mg Cholesterol

Orange French Toast

Golden-Door Yogurt Bran Muffins

1½ cups wheat bran
½ cup boiling water
1⅓ cups whole wheat flour
1¼ teaspoons baking soda
½ teaspoon ground cinnamon
¼ teaspoon salt
¼ teaspoon ground cloves
¼ teaspoon ground nutmeg
1 egg
⅓ cup honey
½ cup DANNON® Plain Nonfat or Lowfat
   Yogurt
3 tablespoons vegetable oil
¾ cup fresh or frozen blueberries

Preheat oven to 350°F. Line muffin cups with paper baking cups. In a medium bowl combine wheat bran and boiling water; let stand 10 minutes to soften. In a large bowl combine flour, baking soda, cinnamon, salt, cloves and nutmeg. In a small bowl combine egg, honey, yogurt and oil; stir well. Add to bran mixture. Add egg mixture all at once to flour mixture; stir just until dry ingredients are moistened. Batter will be stiff. Fold in blueberries.

Fill prepared muffin cups ⅔ full. Bake 20 to 25 minutes or until toothpick inserted into center comes out clean. Serve warm.

12 muffins

Nutritional information per serving:

130 Calories   4.5 g Fat   20 mg Cholesterol

Top to bottom: Lemon Yogurt Raisin Tea Bread (page 8) and Golden-Door Yogurt Bran Muffins

Lemon Yogurt Raisin Tea Bread

1¼ cups all-purpose flour
¾ cup whole wheat flour
4 tablespoons sugar, divided
2 teaspoons baking powder
½ teaspoon baking soda
¼ teaspoon salt
1½ cups DANNON® Lemon Lowfat Yogurt
¼ cup unsalted butter or margarine, melted and cooled slightly
1 egg
¾ cup raisins

Preheat oven to 350°F. Grease an 8½×4½-inch loaf pan. In a large bowl combine flours, 3 tablespoons sugar, baking powder, baking soda and salt. In a medium bowl combine yogurt, butter and egg; stir until well blended. Pour yogurt mixture into flour mixture. Add raisins; stir just until dry ingredients are moistened. Pour into prepared pan and smooth top. Sprinkle surface with remaining 1 tablespoon sugar.

Bake 40 to 45 minutes or until lightly brown and toothpick inserted just off center comes out clean. Cool in pan on wire rack 30 minutes. Remove from pan; cool completely, sugared side up.   *12 servings*

Nutritional information per serving:

190 Calories   5 g Fat   35 mg Cholesterol

Tropical Blend

1 cup DANNON® Plain Nonfat or Lowfat Yogurt
1 cup crushed pineapple in juice, undrained
½ cup orange juice
1 ripe kiwi fruit, peeled and sliced
2 tablespoons wheat germ

In blender container combine yogurt, pineapple, orange juice, kiwi fruit and wheat germ. Cover and blend on high speed until smooth. Serve immediately over ice or in frosted mugs.   *2 servings*

Nutritional information per serving:

210 Calories   1 g Fat   Less than 5 mg Cholesterol

Dannon® Muffins

1½ cups all-purpose flour
¾ cup sugar
2 teaspoons baking powder
1 teaspoon baking soda
½ teaspoon salt
⅔ cup DANNON® Plain Nonfat or Lowfat Yogurt
⅔ cup skim milk
½ cup blueberries or grated apple (optional)

Preheat oven to 400°F. Grease muffin cups or line with paper baking cups. In a large bowl combine flour, sugar, baking powder, baking soda and salt. Gently add yogurt, milk and blueberries; stir just until dry ingredients are moistened.

Fill prepared muffin cups ⅔ full. Bake 18 minutes or until lightly brown and toothpick inserted into center comes out clean. Serve warm.   *12 muffins*

Nutritional information per serving:

120 Calories   2 g Fat   5 mg Cholesterol

Fruit Juicey

1 cup frozen pineapple-orange-banana juice concentrate, thawed
1 cup DANNON® Plain Nonfat or Lowfat Yogurt
¾ cup water
2 tablespoons honey
1 teaspoon vanilla
Ice cubes

In blender container combine juice concentrate, yogurt, water, honey and vanilla. Cover and blend on high speed until smooth. Add enough ice cubes to bring mixture to 6 cup level; process until smooth. Serve immediately.   *6 servings (6 cups)*

Nutritional information per serving:

70 Calories   0 g Fat   Less than 5 mg Cholesterol

Banana Berry Blend

1 cup DANNON® Plain Nonfat or Lowfat
   Yogurt
½ cup orange juice
½ cup fresh or frozen unsweetened
   strawberries
1 ripe banana, sliced
2 tablespoons honey
1 tablespoon wheat germ (optional)

In blender container combine all ingredients. Cover and blend on high speed until smooth. Serve immediately over ice or in frosted mugs.   *2 servings*

Nutritional information per serving:

220 Calories   1 g Fat   Less than 5 mg Cholesterol

Eggs Dannon®

4 eggs
4 thin slices Canadian bacon
1 cup DANNON® Plain Nonfat or Lowfat
   Yogurt
½ teaspoon dry mustard
   Dash ground red pepper
2 English muffins, split and toasted

Spray a large skillet with vegetable cooking spray. Fill half full with water. Bring to a boil; reduce heat until water simmers. Break egg into a small dish and slide into water. Repeat with remaining eggs. Simmer 3 to 5 minutes or until yolks are firm.

In a large skillet over medium-high heat cook bacon 3 to 4 minutes or until heated through, turning once; set aside. In a small saucepan whisk together yogurt, mustard and red pepper. Cook and stir over low heat just until warm. *Do not boil.* Top each English muffin half with bacon slice, egg and ¼ cup sauce. Serve immediately.

4 servings

Nutritional information per serving:

220 Calories   8 g Fat   230 mg Cholesterol

Banana Berry Blend

Blueberry-Lemon Muffins

1¾ cups all-purpose flour
⅓ cup sugar
2½ teaspoons baking powder
¾ teaspoon salt
1 egg, beaten
1 cup DANNON® Plain or Lemon Lowfat
    Yogurt
⅓ cup vegetable oil
2 tablespoons milk
½ to 1 teaspoon grated lemon peel
¾ cup fresh or frozen blueberries

Preheat oven to 400°F. Grease muffin cups or line with paper baking cups. In a large bowl combine flour, sugar, baking powder and salt. In a medium bowl combine egg, yogurt, oil, milk and lemon peel; stir well. Add egg mixture all at once to flour mixture. Stir just until dry ingredients are moistened (batter should be lumpy). Gently fold blueberries into batter.

Fill prepared muffin cups ⅔ full. Bake 20 to 25 minutes or until golden and toothpick inserted into center comes out clean. Serve warm.   *12 muffins*

Nutritional information per serving:

170 Calories   7 g Fat   25 mg Cholesterol

Blueberry-Lemon Muffins

Lemon Yogurt Coffeecake

1/3 cup canola oil
2/3 cup honey
1 egg
3/4 cup cholesterol-free egg substitute
1 1/2 teaspoons lemon extract
1 3/4 cups all-purpose flour
3/4 cup whole wheat pastry flour or whole
    wheat flour
2 1/2 teaspoons baking powder
1 cup DANNON® Lemon Lowfat Yogurt
1 tablespoon grated lemon peel
1 cup coarsely chopped cranberries

Preheat oven to 350°F. Grease and flour a 9-cup kugelhopf or 9-inch bundt pan. In a large bowl beat oil and honey until creamy. Add egg, egg substitute and lemon extract; beat until blended. In a medium bowl combine flours and baking powder; stir into honey mixture alternately with yogurt. Fold in lemon peel and cranberries. Pour into prepared pan; smooth top.

Bake 30 to 35 minutes or until toothpick inserted into center comes out clean. Cool in pan on wire rack. To serve, invert coffeecake onto platter or cake plate.   *12 to 16 servings*

Nutritional information per serving:

230 Calories   7 g Fat   20 mg Cholesterol

Lemon Yogurt Coffeecake

FIT 'N' FRESH SALADS

Crunchy Tuna Waldorf Salad

- 1 can (9¼ ounces) tuna packed in water, drained and flaked
- 1 large apple, cored and chopped
- ⅓ cup chopped celery
- ⅓ cup chopped walnuts
- ⅓ cup raisins, currants or chopped pitted dates
- ½ cup DANNON® Plain Nonfat or Lowfat Yogurt
- ¼ cup mayonnaise or salad dressing Leaf lettuce
- ½ cup shredded Cheddar or Monterey Jack cheese (2 ounces)

In a medium bowl combine tuna, apple, celery, walnuts and raisins; set aside. In a small bowl combine yogurt and mayonnaise. Add to tuna-fruit mixture; toss gently. Cover; chill before serving.

To serve, line 4 salad plates with lettuce leaves. Sprinkle cheese over lettuce. Spoon tuna-fruit mixture on top of cheese.   *4 servings*

Nutritional information per serving:

390 Calories   23 g Fat   65 mg Cholesterol

Crunchy Tuna Waldorf Salad

Shrimp and Snow Pea Salad

¼ pound fresh snow peas, strings removed
2 cups (6 ounces) medium pasta shells
1 cup DANNON® Plain Nonfat or Lowfat
 Yogurt
1 tablespoon red wine vinegar
1 teaspoon minced garlic
½ teaspoon salt
¼ teaspoon pepper
¼ teaspoon dried oregano leaves, crushed
1 pound fully cooked medium shrimp,
 peeled and deveined
6 cherry tomatoes, halved
½ cup red bell pepper strips
¼ cup sliced green onions
 Large lettuce leaves

In a large saucepan bring water to a boil. Add snow peas and boil 1 to 2 minutes or until tender-crisp. Remove from saucepan with slotted spoon; place in ice water to cool quickly. Drain. Add pasta to boiling water; stir well and return to a boil. Reduce heat to medium-high and simmer 10 to 12 minutes, stirring often; drain. Rinse in cold water and drain again.

In a large bowl combine yogurt, vinegar, garlic, salt, pepper and oregano; stir well. Add shrimp, snow peas, pasta, cherry tomatoes, bell pepper and green onions. Toss gently. To serve, line large platter with lettuce leaves; spoon salad over lettuce.   *4 servings (6 cups)*

Nutritional information per serving:
290 Calories   3 g Fat   130 mg Cholesterol

Shrimp and Snow Pea Salad

Greens with Pears and Walnuts

1 cup DANNON® Plain Nonfat or Lowfat
    Yogurt
1 tablespoon walnut or peanut oil
1 tablespoon raspberry vinegar
1 teaspoon sugar
¼ teaspoon salt
¼ teaspoon ground nutmeg
1 head Boston or Bibb lettuce, torn
1 bunch watercress, trimmed and torn
1 bunch arugula, trimmed and torn
1 head Belgian endive, cored and leaves
    separated
2 ripe pears, cored and thinly sliced
¾ cup shredded Swiss cheese (3 ounces)
½ cup finely chopped walnuts, toasted
    Pomegranate seeds (optional)

In a small bowl combine yogurt, oil, vinegar, sugar, salt and nutmeg. Cover; chill 1 hour.

To serve, line 4 plates with greens. Arrange pears and cheese on greens; sprinkle with walnuts. Drizzle dressing over salad. If desired, garnish with pomegranate seeds. *4 servings*

NOTE: If raspberry vinegar is unavailable, substitute white wine vinegar.

Nutritional information per serving:

330 Calories   19 g Fat   20 mg Cholesterol

Gingered Fruit Salad

2 oranges, peeled and sectioned
2 tart apples, cored and chopped
2 peaches, sliced
1 cup strawberry halves
1 cup DANNON® Plain Nonfat or Lowfat
    Yogurt
2 tablespoons packed brown sugar
½ teaspoon ginger

In a large bowl toss oranges, apples, peaches and strawberries. In a small bowl combine yogurt, brown sugar and ginger. Blend well with wire whisk or fork. Toss with fruit.   *8 servings*

Nutritional information per serving:

80 Calories   0 g Fat   Less than 5 mg Cholesterol

Sunflower-Herb Dressing

¼ cup unsalted sunflower nuts
1 clove garlic, crushed
1 cup DANNON® Plain Nonfat or Lowfat
    Yogurt
2 tablespoons milk
1 teaspoon dried basil, crushed
½ teaspoon dried thyme, crushed
⅛ teaspoon dry mustard
⅛ teaspoon pepper

In food processor or blender combine sunflower nuts and garlic. Cover; process to a fine powder (almost a paste). Add yogurt, milk, basil, thyme, dry mustard and pepper. Process until smooth. Cover; chill 2 hours.   *8 servings (about 1 cup)*

Nutritional information per serving:

35 Calories   2 g Fat   Less than 5 mg Cholesterol

Gingered Fruit Salad

Fresh Basil and Pepper Potato Salad

        3 medium potatoes (about 1 pound)
        1 cup DANNON® Plain Nonfat or Lowfat
            Yogurt
        2 tablespoons snipped fresh parsley *or*
            ½ teaspoon dried parsley flakes
        1 tablespoon snipped fresh basil *or*
            1 teaspoon dried basil, crushed
        1 tablespoon sliced green onion
        ½ teaspoon salt
            Several dashes pepper
        ½ cup frozen peas, thawed
        ½ cup chopped red or green bell pepper

In a large saucepan bring water to a boil; add potatoes. Cover and cook 25 to 30 minutes or until tender; drain. Cool. If desired, peel potatoes. Cut potatoes into cubes.

In a large bowl combine yogurt, parsley, basil, green onion, salt and pepper. Add potatoes, peas and bell pepper; stir lightly to coat. Cover; chill several hours before serving.   *5 servings*

Nutritional information per serving:

140 Calories   1 g Fat   Less than 5 mg Cholesterol

Pasta Salad with Parmesan Yogurt Dressing

        8 ounces rotini pasta
        1½ cups DANNON® Plain Nonfat or Lowfat
            Yogurt
        1 cup cubed cooked chicken
        1 cup sliced carrots
        1 cup thin green bell pepper strips
        1 cup broccoli flowerets
        1 cup halved cherry tomatoes
        ½ cup grated Parmesan cheese
        1 tablespoon chopped fresh parsley
        ¼ teaspoon salt
            Dash pepper

Cook pasta according to package directions; drain. Rinse in cold water and drain again. Place in a large bowl. Add yogurt, chicken, carrots, bell pepper, broccoli, tomatoes, cheese, parsley, salt and pepper; toss until well mixed. Serve immediately or cover and chill until ready to serve.

4 servings

Nutritional information per serving:

420 Calories   7 g Fat   45 mg Cholesterol

Moroccan Vegetable Salad

½ **pound small whole mushrooms**
1½ **cups cooked garbanzo beans (chick peas)**
1 **cup pitted large black olives**
12 **cherry tomatoes, halved**
¾ **cup coarsely chopped green onions**
2 **green bell peppers, chopped**
2 **red bell peppers, chopped**
1 **cup DANNON® Plain Nonfat or Lowfat Yogurt**
½ **cup reduced-calorie mayonnaise**
2 **garlic cloves, crushed**
2 **tablespoons olive oil**
1 **tablespoon lemon juice**
1 **teaspoon ground cumin**
⅛ **teaspoon ground turmeric**
Salt and pepper
Lettuce leaves

Steam mushrooms over boiling water 5 minutes; cool. In a large bowl combine mushrooms, garbanzo beans, olives, tomatoes, green onions and bell peppers. Cover; chill 2 hours. In a small bowl combine yogurt, mayonnaise, garlic, olive oil, lemon juice, cumin and turmeric. Season with salt and pepper. Cover; chill 2 hours. Just before serving, lightly toss mushroom mixture with some of dressing. Serve on lettuce leaves. Serve with remaining dressing.

10 servings

Nutritional information per serving:

130 Calories   7 g Fat   10 mg Cholesterol

Honey of a Chicken Salad

4 cups cubed cooked chicken
1½ cups cubed papaya or seedless green grapes
1 cup pecan pieces, toasted
½ cup mayonnaise
¼ cup DANNON® Vanilla Lowfat Yogurt
2 tablespoons honey
1 teaspoon poppy seeds
¼ teaspoon white pepper
1 tablespoon fresh lime juice
Lettuce leaves
Papaya slices and pecan pieces (optional)

In a large bowl combine chicken, papaya and pecan pieces. In a small bowl combine mayonnaise, yogurt, honey, poppy seeds, white pepper and lime juice. Add to chicken mixture. Gently toss to coat. To serve, line 6 plates with lettuce leaves. If desired, fan papaya slices on each plate. Top with chicken salad mixture. If desired, garnish with pecan pieces. *6 servings*

Nutritional information per serving:

560 Calories   33 g Fat   140 mg Cholesterol

Blue Cheese Yogurt Dressing

1 cup DANNON® Plain Nonfat or Lowfat
   Yogurt
4 ounces crumbled blue cheese
½ cup buttermilk
¼ cup minced fresh parsley
1 tablespoon olive oil
1 teaspoon sherry
½ teaspoon pepper

In a small bowl combine all ingredients; stir well. Cover; chill overnight. *14 servings (about 1¾ cups)*

Nutritional information per serving:

50 Calories   4 g Fat   10 mg Cholesterol

Honey of a Chicken Salad

Curried Turkey and Peanut Salad

½ cup DANNON® Plain Nonfat or Lowfat
   Yogurt
¼ cup mayonnaise or salad dressing
1 to 1½ teaspoons curry powder
¼ teaspoon salt
⅛ teaspoon pepper
3 cups chopped cooked turkey or chicken
1 cup halved seedless grapes
½ cup chopped water chestnuts
½ cup chopped red or green bell pepper
   Lettuce leaves
⅓ cup chopped peanuts

In a large bowl combine yogurt, mayonnaise, curry powder, salt and pepper; mix well. Fold in turkey, grapes, water chestnuts and bell pepper. Cover; chill thoroughly before serving.

To serve, line 6 plates with lettuce leaves. Spoon turkey salad over lettuce leaves. Top with chopped peanuts.   *6 servings*

Nutritional information per serving:

280 Calories   15 g Fat   60 mg Cholesterol

Orange Poppy Seed Dressing

1 cup DANNON® Plain or Vanilla Lowfat
   Yogurt
1 tablespoon honey
1 tablespoon frozen orange juice
   concentrate, thawed
1 teaspoon poppy seeds
1 teaspoon finely shredded orange peel

In a medium bowl combine yogurt, honey, orange juice concentrate, poppy seeds and orange peel; stir well. Cover; chill 2 hours.

8 servings (about 1 cup)

Nutritional information per serving:

30 Calories   1 g Fat   Less than 5 mg Cholesterol

Curried Turkey and Peanut Salad

SUPER SNACKS & SANDWICHES

Chunky Salsa Chicken Sandwiches

2½ cups diced cooked chicken
1 cup DANNON® Plain Nonfat or Lowfat Yogurt
¼ cup chunky salsa
½ teaspoon ground cumin
½ cup finely chopped red or green bell pepper
⅓ cup finely chopped fresh cilantro or parsley
⅓ cup finely chopped green onions
3 (6-inch) pita bread rounds, cut in half
Toppings: shredded lettuce, sliced ripe olives, chopped tomatoes and shredded Cheddar cheese

In a large bowl combine chicken, yogurt, salsa and cumin; stir gently. Stir in bell pepper, cilantro and green onions. Line each pita half with lettuce. Spoon chicken salad mixture evenly into pockets; sprinkle remaining toppings over chicken salad mixture. Serve immediately. *6 servings*

NOTE: *If using nonfat yogurt, drain excess liquid by placing yogurt in a coffee filter for 5 minutes.*

Nutritional information per serving:

300 Calories   6.5 g Fat   90 mg Cholesterol

Chunky Salsa Chicken Sandwiches

Mexican Chicken Skewers with Spicy Yogurt Sauce

1 package (1.25 ounces) taco seasoning mix,
    divided
6 boneless skinless chicken breast halves
    (about 1½ pounds), cut into 1-inch cubes
1 large clove garlic
¼ teaspoon salt
2 tablespoons olive oil
1 cup DANNON® Plain Nonfat or Lowfat
    Yogurt
1 red bell pepper, cut into chunks
1 green bell pepper, cut into chunks
1 yellow bell pepper, cut into chunks

In a large bowl combine 3 tablespoons seasoning mix and chicken; toss to coat well. Cover; chill 2 hours.

To make Spicy Yogurt Sauce, in a mortar and pestle or with a large knife press garlic and salt together until a smooth paste forms. Place in a small bowl with olive oil; mix well. Stir in yogurt and remaining taco seasoning mix. Cover; chill 30 minutes before serving.

Thread chicken onto skewers alternately with peppers; grill over hot coals 10 to 12 minutes, turning occasionally. Serve with Spicy Yogurt Sauce.   *12 servings*

NOTE: *If using wooden skewers, soak them in water 30 minutes before serving. This will prevent skewers from charring and crumbling.*

Nutritional information per serving:
140 Calories   4.5 g Fat   50 mg Cholesterol

Mexican Chicken Skewers with Spicy Yogurt Sauce

Spicy Bean Tostadas

1 can (15½ ounces) red kidney beans,
    drained and rinsed
1 can (14½ ounces) yellow hominy, drained
1 can (10 ounces) tomatoes with green chile
    peppers
1 can (8 ounces) tomato sauce
½ cup sliced celery
½ cup chopped onion
1 tablespoon snipped fresh parsley
1 teaspoon chili powder
½ teaspoon sugar
1 tablespoon cold water
2 teaspoons cornstarch
4 (6- to 7-inch) corn or flour tortillas
2 cups shredded lettuce
2 medium tomatoes, chopped
½ cup shredded Cheddar cheese (2 ounces)
1 cup DANNON® Plain Nonfat or Lowfat
    Yogurt
    Taco sauce or salsa (optional)

In a large saucepan combine kidney beans, hominy, tomatoes with
green chile peppers, tomato sauce, celery, onion, parsley, chili
powder and sugar. Bring to a boil; reduce heat. Cover; simmer 10
minutes. Combine cold water and cornstarch; add to saucepan. Cook
and stir until thickened and bubbly; cook and stir 2 minutes more.

Preheat oven to 350°F. Place tortillas in a single layer on baking
sheet. Bake 10 to 15 minutes or until crisp. Place each tortilla on a
serving plate. Divide bean mixture among tortillas, then sprinkle
with lettuce, tomatoes and cheese. Top with yogurt. If desired, serve
with taco sauce.   *4 servings*

Nutritional information per serving:

550 Calories   7 g Fat   15 mg Cholesterol

Spicy Bean Tostadas

Splendid Spinach Dip

**2 cups DANNON® Plain Nonfat or Lowfat
    Yogurt**
**1 package (10 ounces) frozen chopped
    spinach, thawed and squeezed dry**
⅓ cup finely chopped fresh onion
2 tablespoons reduced-calorie mayonnaise
**1 package (1.4 ounces) instant vegetable soup
    mix**
Assorted fresh vegetable dippers

In a medium bowl combine yogurt, spinach, onion, mayonnaise and
vegetable soup mix; mix well. Serve immediately or cover and chill
up to 3 hours. Serve with vegetable dippers.

24 servings (about 3 cups)

Nutritional information per serving dip:

10 Calories   0 g Fat   Less than 5 mg Cholesterol

Chunky Chili Dip

**⅔ cup DANNON® Plain Nonfat or Lowfat
    Yogurt**
⅓ cup mayonnaise or salad dressing
¼ cup finely chopped green bell pepper
¼ cup chili sauce
2 tablespoons finely chopped green onion
1 tablespoon prepared horseradish
Assorted fresh vegetable dippers

In a medium bowl combine yogurt, mayonnaise, bell pepper, chili
sauce, green onion and horseradish; mix well. Cover; chill before
serving. Serve with vegetable dippers.   *12 servings (about 1½ cups)*

Nutritional information per serving dip:

60 Calories   5 g Fat   Less than 5 mg Cholesterol

*Clockwise from top left: Splendid Spinach Dip,
Chunky Chili Dip and Creamy Tarragon Dip* **(page 38)**

Creamy Tarragon Dip

1 cup DANNON® Plain Nonfat or Lowfat
Yogurt
1 cup mayonnaise or salad dressing
1 tablespoon chopped green onion
1 tablespoon snipped fresh parsley
2 teaspoons lemon juice
½ teaspoon dried tarragon, crushed
Dash freshly ground pepper
Assorted fresh vegetable dippers

In a medium bowl combine yogurt, mayonnaise, green onion, parsley, lemon juice, tarragon and pepper; mix well. Cover; chill up to 24 hours before serving. Serve with vegetable dippers.

16 servings (about 2 cups)

Nutritional information per serving dip:

110 Calories   11 g Fat   10 mg Cholesterol

Black Bean Chicken Burritos

1 cup DANNON® Plain Nonfat or Lowfat
Yogurt
¼ to ½ teaspoon ground cumin
¼ to ½ teaspoon ground ginger
¼ teaspoon salt
1 cup chopped onions
1 tablespoon olive oil
1 can (15 ounces) black beans or pinto beans,
rinsed and drained
1 can (4 ounces) chopped green chiles,
drained
8 (10-inch) flour tortillas, warmed
2 cans (6¾ ounces *each*) chunk white
chicken, drained and flaked
1 can (8 ounces) pineapple tidbits in juice,
drained
1 cup shredded Monterey Jack or colby
cheese (4 ounces)

In a small bowl combine yogurt, cumin, ginger and salt; stir well and set aside. In a large skillet cook and stir onions in oil until tender. Add beans. Using wooden spoon or potato masher, mash beans. Stir in green chiles. Remove from heat.

Preheat oven to 350°F. Place 3 tablespoons bean mixture in center of each tortilla; top with chicken, pineapple tidbits and cheese. Fold sides of tortilla over filling, overlapping to form a cone shape. Secure each burrito with a toothpick. Place burritos on baking sheet. Cover lightly with aluminum foil. Bake 15 to 20 minutes or until hot. Remove toothpicks. Spoon yogurt mixture over burritos.

8 servings

Nutritional information per serving:

500 Calories   12 g Fat   35 mg Cholesterol

Chili Pizzas

**1 cup DANNON® Plain Nonfat or Lowfat
   Yogurt**
4 (8-inch) flour tortillas
1 cup canned chili without beans
1 tablespoon instant minced onion
1 cup shredded Cheddar cheese (4 ounces)
1 cup shredded iceberg lettuce
1 large tomato, seeded and diced

Spoon yogurt into large strainer lined with double thickness of cheesecloth or a coffee filter. Place bowl beneath, but not touching strainer to catch liquid. Let stand at room temperature 15 minutes. Discard liquid.

Preheat oven to 400°F. Place tortillas on lightly greased baking sheet. Bake 3 minutes, turning once. In a small bowl combine chili and onion. Spread ¼ cup chili mixture on each crisped tortilla leaving a ½-inch border around edge. Divide cheese evenly among tortillas. Return to oven. Bake 5 minutes or until cheese is melted. Top evenly with lettuce, tomato and drained yogurt. Serve immediately.

4 servings

Nutritional information per serving:

270 Calories   13 g Fat   30 mg Cholesterol

Layered Guacamole

3 ripe avocados, peeled and mashed
1 tablespoon lemon juice
1 package (1.4 ounces) onion soup mix
¾ cup DANNON® Plain Nonfat or Lowfat
    Yogurt
2 cups shredded Colby-Jack cheese
    (8 ounces)
3 medium tomatoes, seeded and diced
¾ cup sliced ripe olives
    Salsa
    Chopped fresh cilantro or parsley
    Tortilla chips

In a medium bowl combine avocados and lemon juice. Stir in onion soup mix and yogurt; mix well. Spread avocado mixture onto a round 10- to 12-inch glass serving platter. Top with cheese, tomatoes, olives, salsa and cilantro. Serve with tortilla chips.   *8 servings*

Nutritional information per serving guacamole:

300 Calories   22 g Fat   30 mg Cholesterol

Savory Dijon Chicken Spread

1 cup finely chopped cooked chicken
4 ounces cream cheese, softened
3 tablespoons finely chopped green onion
1 tablespoon Dijon-style mustard
1½ teaspoons curry powder
½ cup DANNON® Plain Nonfat or Lowfat
    Yogurt
    Melba rounds or rye bread

In a medium bowl combine chicken, cream cheese, green onion, mustard and curry powder; mix well. Stir in yogurt. Serve with melba rounds or rye bread.   *14 servings (about 1¾ cups)*

Nutritional information per serving spread:

60 Calories   4 g Fat   20 mg Cholesterol

Layered Guacamole

Swiss 'n' Cheddar Cheeseball

1 package (8 ounces) cream cheese, softened
½ cup DANNON® Plain Nonfat or Lowfat
   Yogurt
2 cups shredded Swiss cheese (8 ounces)
2 cups shredded Cheddar cheese (8 ounces)
½ cup finely chopped onion
1 jar (2 ounces) diced pimiento, undrained
2 tablespoons sweet pickle relish
10 slices bacon, crisp-cooked, drained,
   crumbled and divided
½ cup finely chopped pecans, divided
¼ cup snipped fresh parsley
1 tablespoon poppy seeds
   Assorted crackers

In a large bowl beat cream cheese and yogurt until fluffy. Beat in Swiss cheese, Cheddar cheese, onion, undrained pimiento, pickle relish, half the bacon and ¼ cup pecans. If desired, season with salt and pepper. Cover; chill until firm. Shape into 1 large or 2 small balls on waxed paper; set aside.

In a small bowl combine remaining bacon, remaining ¼ cup pecans, parsley and poppy seeds; turn out onto clean sheet of waxed paper. Roll ball in bacon mixture to coat. Cover in plastic wrap; chill. Serve with crackers.   *24 servings*

Nutritional information per serving cheeseball:

150 Calories   12 g Fat   30 mg Cholesterol

Swiss 'n' Cheddar Cheeseball

SENSATIONAL SOUPS & SIDES

Chilled Potatoes in Creamy Herb Sauce

4 red new potatoes, unpeeled and scrubbed
1 cup frozen peas, thawed
½ cup chopped green bell pepper
1½ cups DANNON® Plain Nonfat or Lowfat Yogurt
2 tablespoons snipped fresh parsley
2 tablespoons sliced green onion
1 teaspoon dried basil leaves, crushed
¼ teaspoon salt
Dash white pepper

In a medium saucepan bring small amount of water to a boil. Add potatoes; cook, covered, 25 to 30 minutes or until tender. Drain and cool. Slice and place in a large bowl. Toss with peas and bell pepper. Add yogurt, parsley, green onion, basil, salt and white pepper. Toss gently to coat. Cover; chill until ready to serve. *8 servings*

Nutritional information per serving:

100 Calories   0 g Fat   Less than 5 mg Cholesterol

Chilled Potatoes in Creamy Herb Sauce

Creamed Peas

1 cup DANNON® Plain Nonfat or Lowfat
    Yogurt
2 tablespoons all-purpose flour
2 tablespoons finely chopped fresh dill weed
    or 1 teaspoon dried dill weed
1 jar (2 ounces) diced pimiento, drained
1/2 teaspoon salt
1/4 teaspoon pepper
1 1/2 cups fresh or frozen English peas
3 tablespoons chicken broth

In a small bowl combine yogurt, flour, dill weed, pimiento, salt and pepper; stir until smooth. Set aside.

In a small saucepan combine peas and broth; cover and bring to a boil. Reduce heat and simmer 5 minutes or until peas are tender. Stir in yogurt mixture; cook over low heat until thickened, stirring constantly. *4 servings*

Nutritional information per serving:

90 Calories   0 g Fat   Less than 5 mg Cholesterol

Bean Stuffed Green Chiles

1 cup DANNON® Plain Nonfat or Lowfat
    Yogurt
1/2 teaspoon ground cumin
1/4 teaspoon salt
2 cloves garlic, minced
1 tablespoon corn oil
1/2 cup minced green onions
1 can (16 ounces) pinto beans, drained
1/2 cup minced fresh cilantro
8 whole fresh mild green chiles, roasted and
    peeled*
    Red Pepper Sauce (recipe follows)

In a small bowl combine yogurt, cumin and salt. Cover; chill until ready to serve.

In a medium skillet over medium-high heat cook and stir garlic in oil 1 minute. Add green onions; cook and stir 2 minutes. Add pinto beans; reduce heat to low. Mash beans with a potato masher or wooden spoon until chunky. Stir in cilantro.

Preheat oven to 325°F. Beginning at stem end, make a lengthwise cut down each chile; open chile flat. Divide bean mixture evenly among the chiles. Gently shape bean mixture to fit chiles. Arrange chiles in 11×7-inch baking dish. Bake 15 to 20 minutes or until thoroughly heated. Spoon Red Pepper Sauce onto 4 serving plates; arrange 2 stuffed chiles on each plate. Top with yogurt mixture.   *4 servings*

*To roast and peel fresh chiles, place on foil-lined broiler rack; roast 2 to 3 inches from heat or until evenly blistered and charred, turning as needed. Immediately place chiles in plastic bag; close bag. Let stand in bag 20 minutes. Peel each chile under cold running water, rubbing and pulling off charred skin. Slit chile open lengthwise using scissors or knife. Carefully pull out and discard seeds and veins. Rinse chiles well; pat dry with paper towels.

Red Pepper Sauce

> **3 large red bell peppers, coarsely chopped**
> **2 cloves garlic, minced**
> **2 tablespoons olive oil**
> **1 tablespoon balsamic vinegar**
> **½ teaspoon freshly ground pepper**
> **1 cup DANNON® Plain Nonfat or Lowfat**
> **Yogurt**

In a large skillet over medium-low heat cook and stir bell peppers and garlic in oil 15 minutes or until tender. Cool.

In food processor or blender combine bell pepper mixture, vinegar and ground pepper. Process until smooth; set aside. Spoon yogurt into strainer lined with double thickness of cheesecloth or a coffee filter. Place bowl beneath, but not touching strainer to catch liquid. Let stand at room temperature 15 minutes. Scrape yogurt into a small bowl. Discard liquid. Add pepper mixture to yogurt; stir well.

Nutritional information per serving:
320 Calories   11 g Fat   Less than 5 mg Cholesterol

Carrots and Raisins Revisited

2 cups DANNON® Plain Nonfat or Lowfat
    Yogurt
1 tablespoon packed brown sugar
¼ teaspoon grated orange peel
2 tablespoons orange juice
¼ teaspoon ground nutmeg or cardamom
    Pinch salt
6 to 7 medium carrots, peeled and coarsely
    shredded (3 cups)
¼ cup raisins
3 tablespoons chopped cashews, almonds or
    pecans

Spoon yogurt into large strainer lined with double thickness of cheesecloth or a coffee filter. Place bowl beneath, but not touching strainer to catch liquid. Chill 1½ hours. Scrape yogurt into a medium bowl. Discard liquid. Add brown sugar, orange peel and juice, nutmeg and salt; stir until smooth. Add carrots and raisins; toss to coat. Cover; chill 20 to 30 minutes before serving. Just before serving, sprinkle with cashews. *6 servings (3 cups)*

Nutritional information per serving:

140 Calories   4 g Fat   5 mg Cholesterol

Texas Potato Topper

1 cup DANNON® Plain Nonfat or Lowfat
    Yogurt
⅓ cup mild or medium chunky salsa
⅓ cup chopped stuffed green olives

In a small bowl combine yogurt, salsa and olives. Cover; chill until ready to serve. To serve, spoon onto baked potato halves.

10 servings

Nutritional information per 1 tablespoon serving:

10 Calories   0 g Fat   Less than 5 mg Cholesterol

Carrots and Raisins Revisited

Salinas Valley Potato Topper

1 tablespoon margarine or butter
½ cup chopped fresh broccoli flowerets
1 cup DANNON® Plain Nonfat or Lowfat
    Yogurt
¼ cup shredded part-skim mozzarella cheese
    (1 ounce)
Paprika

In a small heavy saucepan over medium heat melt margarine. Add
broccoli; cook and stir just until tender. Remove from heat. Stir in
yogurt and mozzarella. To serve, spoon onto baked potato halves
and sprinkle with paprika.   *10 servings*

Nutritional information per 1 tablespoon serving:
10 Calories   0 g Fat   Less than 5 mg Cholesterol

Little Italy Potato Topper

1 cup DANNON® Plain Nonfat or Lowfat
    Yogurt
½ cup tomato, chopped
2 tablespoons grated Parmesan cheese
1 tablespoon chopped fresh basil leaves *or*
    ½ teaspoon dried basil
1 tablespoon fresh oregano *or* ¼ teaspoon
    dried oregano
¼ teaspoon salt

In a small bowl combine yogurt, tomato, cheese, basil, oregano and
salt. Cover; chill until ready to serve. To serve, spoon onto baked
potato halves.   *10 servings*

Nutritional information per 1 tablespoon serving:
10 Calories   0 g Fat   Less than 5 mg Cholesterol

Clockwise from top left: Salinas Valley Potato Topper, Dakota Potato Topper
(page 52) *and Little Italy Potato Topper*

Dakota Potato Topper

1 cup DANNON® Plain Nonfat or Lowfat
  Yogurt
3 tablespoons bacon bits
2 teaspoons prepared white horseradish

In a small bowl combine yogurt, bacon bits and horseradish. Cover;
chill until ready to serve. To serve, spoon onto baked potato halves.

8 servings

Nutritional information per 1 tablespoon serving:

10 Calories   0 g Fat   Less than 5 mg Cholesterol

Savory Mashed Potatoes

1 tablespoon olive oil
1 tablespoon minced garlic
4 cups water
4 medium russet potatoes, peeled and cut
  into quarters (2 to 2¼ pounds)
1 cup DANNON® Plain Nonfat or Lowfat
  Yogurt
¼ cup milk
¼ cup sliced scallions or green onions
1 teaspoon salt
¼ teaspoon freshly ground pepper

In a large heavy saucepan or Dutch oven heat oil over medium-low
heat. Add garlic; cook and stir 1 minute, stirring constantly, until
fragrant but not browned. Add water and potatoes. Cover and bring
to a boil over high heat. Reduce heat to medium-low and simmer 15
to 20 minutes or until potatoes are very tender. Drain well. Return
potatoes to saucepan and mash. Add yogurt and milk and stir until
creamy. Stir in scallions, salt and pepper. Serve immediately.

6 to 8 servings (5 cups)

Nutritional information per serving:

110 Calories   2 g Fat   Less than 5 mg Cholesterol

Chilled Minted Cucumber Yogurt Soup

        2 cucumbers
        ½ small onion, cut into chunks
        1 clove garlic
        2 cups DANNON® Plain Nonfat or Lowfat
            Yogurt, divided
        3 tablespoons thinly sliced fresh mint leaves
        ½ teaspoon salt
        ⅛ teaspoon freshly ground pepper
            Pinch ground red pepper
        4 thin cucumber slices (optional)

Peel cucumbers and halve lengthwise. Scoop out seeds with spoon
and discard. Cut cucumbers into chunks. Place cucumbers, onion
and garlic in food processor. Process until smooth. Add 1 cup yogurt
and process until smooth. Scrape into a medium bowl or soup
tureen. Stir in remaining 1 cup yogurt, mint, salt, pepper and ground
red pepper. Cover; chill at least 2 hours before serving. To serve,
ladle into 4 soup bowls and garnish each with a cucumber slice.

4 servings (about 3½ cups)

Nutritional information per serving:

100 Calories   2 g Fat   10 mg Cholesterol

Cauliflower with Creamy Chive Sauce

        1 head cauliflower, washed
        1 cup DANNON® Plain Nonfat or Lowfat
            Yogurt
        1 tablespoon chopped fresh chives *or*
            ½ teaspoon dried chives
        1 teaspoon dry mustard

Steam cauliflower, covered, over boiling water 15 to 20 minutes or
until tender. In a small bowl combine yogurt, chives and mustard.
Blend well with wire whisk or fork. Spoon over cooked cauliflower,
allowing steam to heat sauce.   *6 servings*

Nutritional information per serving:

40 Calories   0.5 g Fat   Less than 5 mg Cholesterol

Satin Salmon Chowder

1 tablespoon margarine or butter
½ cup chopped onion
1 clove garlic, minced
2 cups water
1 cup diced peeled potatoes
1 envelope (about 3.5 grams) low-sodium
    instant chicken bouillon
1 can (8 ounces) corn kernels, drained
1 can (7½ ounces) salmon, drained and
    flaked
¼ cup diced green or red bell pepper
¼ teaspoon freshly ground pepper
2 cups DANNON® Plain Nonfat or Lowfat
    Yogurt
¼ cup all-purpose flour

In a large saucepan melt margarine over medium heat. Add onion and garlic; cook and stir 2 to 3 minutes or just until tender. Stir in water, potatoes and chicken bouillon. Bring to a boil and simmer, stirring occasionally, 4 to 5 minutes or until potatoes are tender. Reduce heat to low. Add corn, salmon, bell pepper and ground pepper. *Do not boil.*

In a medium bowl, combine yogurt and flour; blend well. Gradually add to soup, stirring constantly, until smooth and slightly thickened.

4 servings (about 5 cups)

Nutritional information per serving:

260 Calories   7 g Fat   20 mg Cholesterol

Satin Salmon Chowder

ENTICING ENTRÉES

Yogurt-Chicken Marinade

½ cup low-sodium chicken broth
½ cup dry white wine
¾ cup sliced leeks
2 tablespoons lemon juice
½ teaspoon grated lemon peel
¼ teaspoon ground allspice
4 boneless skinless chicken breast
halves (about 1 pound), trimmed
of all visible fat
1 cup DANNON® Plain Nonfat or Lowfat
Yogurt
1 tablespoon Dijon-style mustard
1 tablespoon snipped fresh parsley

In a large shallow dish combine chicken broth, wine, leeks, lemon juice, lemon peel and allspice; add chicken. Cover; chill several hours or overnight. Remove chicken from marinade and place on broiler pan; reserve marinade. Broil 4 to 6 inches from heat 8 to 12 minutes or until lightly brown. *Preheat oven to 350°F.* Place chicken in shallow baking pan; set aside. In a small saucepan bring reserved marinade to a boil; reduce heat and simmer, covered, 5 minutes. Cool 10 minutes. Whisk in yogurt, mustard and parsley. Spoon over chicken. Bake 15 minutes or until chicken is no longer pink in center.

4 servings

Nutritional information per serving:
260 Calories   5 g Fat   100 mg Cholesterol

Yogurt-Chicken Marinade

Italian Ham Lasagna

6 lasagna noodles (4 ounces)
1 package (10 ounces) frozen chopped
    spinach
1 cup milk
2 tablespoons cornstarch
1 tablespoon dried minced onion
½ cup DANNON® Plain Nonfat or Lowfat
    Yogurt
1 cup diced fully cooked ham
½ teaspoon Italian seasoning, crushed
¼ cup grated Parmesan cheese
1 cup lowfat cottage cheese
1 cup shredded mozzarella cheese

Cook noodles according to package directions; rinse and drain. Set aside. Cook spinach according to package directions; drain well. Set aside.

Preheat oven to 375°F. In a large saucepan combine milk, cornstarch and onion. Cook and stir until thickened and bubbly; cook and stir 2 minutes more. Remove from heat. Stir in yogurt. Spread 2 tablespoons of yogurt sauce evenly on bottom of 10×6-inch baking dish. Stir ham and Italian seasoning into remaining sauce. Place 3 lasagna noodles in dish. (Trim noodles to fit, if necessary.) Spread with ⅓ of sauce. Layer spinach on top. Sprinkle with Parmesan. Layer another ⅓ of sauce, the cottage cheese and ½ of mozzarella cheese. Place remaining noodles on top of cheese layer. Top with remaining sauce and mozzarella. Bake 30 to 35 minutes or until heated through. Let stand 10 minutes before serving. *6 servings*

Nutritional information per serving:

270 Calories   9 g Fat   50 mg Cholesterol

Italian Ham Lasagna

Chicken Paprikash

¾ cup DANNON® Plain Nonfat or Lowfat
   Yogurt
2 tablespoons olive oil
2 cups sliced onions
1 cup red bell pepper strips
1½ teaspoons minced garlic
1 tablespoon plus 1½ teaspoons all-purpose
   flour
1 to 2 teaspoons Hungarian paprika
1 cup chicken broth
1 pound chicken cutlets, trimmed of all
   visible fat, cut into 2×1-inch strips
½ teaspoon salt
¼ teaspoon pepper
   Hot cooked noodles (optional)
   Snipped fresh parsley (optional)

Spoon yogurt into large strainer lined with double thickness of cheesecloth or a coffee filter. Place bowl beneath, but not touching strainer to catch liquid. Let stand at room temperature 15 minutes. Scrape yogurt into a small bowl. Discard liquid.

In a large heavy saucepan or Dutch oven heat oil over medium-low heat. Add onions, bell pepper and garlic; stir well. Cook, covered, 10 to 15 minutes or until tender, stirring occasionally. Reduce heat if vegetables start to brown. Sprinkle in flour and paprika; cook uncovered 1 minute, stirring constantly. (Pan will seem very dry.)

Add broth; increase heat to medium-high. Cook, stirring constantly, until sauce thickens and boils. Add chicken; stir well and return to a boil. Reduce heat to low; simmer, covered, 8 to 10 minutes or until chicken is cooked through. Remove from heat; uncover and let cool slightly. Stir a little of hot chicken sauce into yogurt then slowly add yogurt to chicken, stirring constantly. Stir in salt and pepper. If desired, serve over hot cooked noodles and garnish with parsley.

4 servings

Nutritional information per serving:

290 Calories   11 g Fat   75 mg Cholesterol

Chicken Paprikash

Scandinavian Meatballs

1½ cups DANNON® Plain Nonfat or Lowfat
    Yogurt, divided
½ cup soft bread crumbs
1 pound lean ground beef
1 egg
¼ cup finely chopped onion
¼ teaspoon salt (optional)
2 tablespoons all-purpose flour
1 envelope (about 3.5 grams) instant beef
    broth mix
1 teaspoon Worcestershire sauce
    Snipped fresh parsley (optional)

In a large bowl combine ½ cup yogurt and bread crumbs; let stand 5 minutes. Add ground beef, egg, onion and salt. Mix well and shape into 1¼-inch meatballs. Spray a large nonstick skillet with vegetable cooking spray. Cook meatballs over medium heat until brown and cooked through, turning often; drain. Wipe skillet dry.

In a small bowl, combine 1 cup yogurt, flour, beef broth mix and Worcestershire sauce until smooth. Add to skillet. Cook over medium-low heat, stirring constantly, until thickened. *Do not boil.* Reduce heat to low. Add meatballs; mix with sauce and cook until just heated through. If desired, garnish with parsley.   *6 servings*

Nutritional information per serving:

190 Calories   7 g Fat   100 mg Cholesterol

Scandinavian Meatballs

Lean Beef Stroganoff

3 tablespoons margarine, divided
¾ pound beef tenderloin, sliced into thin
    strips
1 pound sliced mushrooms (6 cups)
¼ cup finely chopped onion
¼ cup dry white wine or apple juice
¼ teaspoon salt
   Dash pepper
   Dash ground nutmeg
1 cup DANNON® Plain Nonfat or Lowfat
    Yogurt
2 tablespoons all-purpose flour
12 ounces wide egg noodles
   Tomato slices (optional)

In a large skillet melt 1 tablespoon margarine over medium-high heat. Add beef; cook and stir until brown. Push to one side of skillet. Add remaining 2 tablespoons margarine. Add mushrooms and onion; cook and stir until tender. Mix with beef. Reduce heat to medium-low. Add wine, salt, pepper and nutmeg; cook 2 to 3 minutes or until hot.

In a small bowl whisk together yogurt and flour until smooth. Stir into beef mixture; cook and stir until heated through. *Do not boil.* Meanwhile, cook noodles according to package directions; rinse and drain well. Serve stroganoff over hot cooked noodles. If desired, garnish with tomato slices.   *6 servings*

NOTE: *If desired, substitute chicken for beef called for in recipe; prepare as directed.*

Nutritional information per serving:

310 Calories   10 g Fat   50 mg Cholesterol

Lean Beef Stroganoff

Confetti Fettucine Dannon®

    12 ounces fettucine noodles
    ¼ cup margarine, softened
    1½ cups DANNON® Plain Nonfat or Lowfat
        Yogurt
    ½ cup grated Parmesan cheese
    ½ cup grated carrots
    2 tablespoons snipped fresh parsley
    ¼ teaspoon salt
        Dash pepper

In a large saucepan cook pasta according to package directions; rinse and drain well. Return pasta to saucepan. Add margarine; toss until melted. Add yogurt, cheese, carrots, parsley, salt and pepper. Toss to coat pasta. Serve immediately.   *6 servings*

Nutritional information per serving:

350 Calories   11 g Fat   10 mg Cholesterol

Mustard Pork Chops

    2 tablespoons Dijon-style mustard
    4 pork loin chops, cut ½-inch thick (about
        1¼ pounds)
    ¼ cup fine dry bread crumbs
    2 tablespoons cornmeal
    1 tablespoon whole wheat flour
    ⅓ cup DANNON® Plain Nonfat or Lowfat
        Yogurt
    1 tablespoon chutney, chopped

Preheat oven to 350°F. Spread mustard on all surfaces of chops. In a medium bowl combine bread crumbs, cornmeal and flour. Coat chops with crumb mixture. Place chops in 9×9-inch baking pan.

Bake 30 to 40 minutes or until chops are no longer pink and coating is lightly browned. In a small bowl combine yogurt and chutney; spoon over chops.   *4 servings*

Nutritional information per serving:

230 Calories   10 g Fat   50 mg Cholesterol

Tandoori-Style Chicken

1 cup DANNON® Plain Nonfat or Lowfat
    Yogurt
3 tablespoons distilled white vinegar
2 teaspoons minced garlic
1¾ teaspoons garam masala*
1¼ teaspoons ground ginger
¼ teaspoon ground red pepper
6 boneless skinless chicken breast halves
    (about 1¾ pounds), trimmed of all
    visible fat
1¼ teaspoons salt
3 teaspoons olive oil, divided
2 cups sliced onions

In a large glass bowl combine yogurt, vinegar, garlic, garam masala, ginger and red pepper. Cut 4½-inch-deep diagonal slashes in top of each chicken breast. Sprinkle salt in slashes. Add chicken to yogurt mixture. Cover; chill at least 8 hours or overnight.

Preheat oven to 375°F. Brush 13×9-inch baking dish with 1 teaspoon oil. Remove chicken from marinade and arrange in a single layer, cut side up, in baking dish. Spoon some of the marinade over chicken; discard remainder. Sprinkle onions over chicken and drizzle with remaining 2 teaspoons oil. Bake 25 to 30 minutes or until chicken is no longer pink. Place chicken under broiler 3 to 5 minutes to brown onions. Serve immediately.   *6 servings*

*Garam masala is available in most Indian specialty shops or make your own from common kitchen spices. In a small bowl combine 1½ teaspoons ground cumin, 1 teaspoon ground coriander, 1 teaspoon ground cardamom, 1 teaspoon pepper, ¼ teaspoon ground bay leaves and a pinch of ground cloves. (If ground bay leaves are not available, grind whole leaves to a fine powder with a mortar and pestle.)

Nutritional information per serving:

250 Calories   7 g Fat   100 mg Cholesterol

Creamy Chicken Primavera

2 cups water
1 cup diced carrots
1 cup broccoli flowerets
1 cup tri-color rotini pasta
½ pound cooked chicken, cut into cubes
½ cup DANNON® Plain Nonfat or Lowfat Yogurt
¼ cup finely chopped green onions (green part only)
2 tablespoons plus 2 teaspoons reduced-calorie mayonnaise
2 tablespoons grated Parmesan cheese
½ teaspoon dried basil, crushed
⅛ teaspoon pepper
Carrot curls (optional)

In a medium saucepan combine water, carrots and broccoli. Cook, covered, 10 to 15 minutes or until tender-crisp; drain. Cook pasta according to package directions; rinse and drain. In a large bowl combine pasta, carrots and broccoli. Toss gently.

In a small bowl combine chicken, yogurt, green onions, mayonnaise, cheese, basil and pepper; mix well. Add to pasta mixture. Toss gently to combine. Cover; chill several hours. If desired, garnish with carrot curls.   *4 servings*

Nutritional information per serving:

290 Calories   10 g Fat   60 mg Cholesterol

Creamy Chicken Primavera

Grilled Salmon with Creamy Tarragon Sauce

1 cup DANNON® Plain Nonfat or Lowfat
  Yogurt
1 tablespoon reduced-calorie mayonnaise
¼ cup minced green onions
1 tablespoon minced fresh tarragon or dill
  weed
2 teaspoons lime juice
1 teaspoon hot pepper sauce
12- to 16-ounce salmon fillet (1-inch thick),
  skinned
1 tablespoon olive oil

In a small glass bowl combine yogurt, mayonnaise, green onions, tarragon, lime juice and hot pepper sauce. Cover; chill at least 1 hour.

Cut salmon into 4 equal portions; brush with olive oil. Grill salmon over medium-hot coals 5 minutes on each side or until fish flakes easily with fork. Serve with tarragon sauce.   *4 servings*

NOTE: Fish may be broiled 4 to 6 inches from heat source 3 to 4 minutes on each side or until fish flakes easily with fork.

Nutritional information per serving:

240 Calories   11.5 g Fat   65 mg Cholesterol

Grilled Salmon with Creamy Tarragon Sauce

Broccoli-Tuna Pasta Toss

5 ounces medium pasta shells
1 package (10 ounces) frozen cut broccoli
1 can (10¾ ounces) condensed cream of
    chicken soup
1 can (8 ounces) sliced water chestnuts,
    drained
½ cup DANNON® Plain Nonfat or Lowfat
    Yogurt
½ cup shredded Cheddar cheese (2 ounces)
1 teaspoon Worcestershire sauce
¼ teaspoon garlic powder
1 can (9¼ ounces) tuna packed in water,
    drained and flaked

Cook pasta according to package directions, adding frozen broccoli
the last 5 to 7 minutes of cooking; drain well. Return pasta and
broccoli to saucepan; cover and keep warm.

In a medium bowl combine soup, water chestnuts, yogurt, cheese,
Worcestershire sauce and garlic powder. Stir soup mixture into
saucepan with drained pasta and broccoli. Gently fold in tuna, being
careful not to break up large pieces. Cook over medium-low heat
about 5 minutes or until heated through, stirring once or twice. Serve
immediately.   *5 servings*

Nutritional information per serving:

320 Calories   9 g Fat   50 mg Cholesterol

Broccoli-Tuna Pasta Toss

DESERVING DESSERTS

Apricot Mousse

4 cups DANNON® Vanilla Lowfat Yogurt
2 cans (16 to 17 ounces *each*) apricot halves in
heavy syrup, drained
1 tablespoon sugar
1½ teaspoons orange-flavored liqueur
(optional)
1 cup fresh blueberries
4 strawberries
Mint leaves (optional)

Spoon yogurt into large strainer lined with double thickness of cheesecloth or a coffee filter. Place bowl beneath, but not touching strainer to catch liquid. Cover; chill 24 hours.

Scrape yogurt into a medium bowl. Discard liquid. Place apricots in a food processor or blender. Process until smooth. In a large bowl combine apricot purée, drained yogurt, sugar and liqueur; mix well. Cover; chill at least 30 minutes.

To serve, spoon blueberries into 6 wine glasses or dessert dishes, reserving a few berries for the top. Spoon mousse over berries. Hull strawberries and slice thinly. Top each serving of mousse with a few slices. Sprinkle with remaining blueberries and garnish each with a mint leaf.   *6 servings*

Nutritional information per serving:

200 Calories   3 g Fat   5 mg Cholesterol

Apricot Mousse

Chocolate Silk Pie

1 envelope unflavored gelatin
¼ cup cold water
1 cup DANNON® Plain Nonfat or Lowfat
  Yogurt
1 cup skim milk
2 teaspoons vanilla
1 package (4-serving size) instant chocolate
  pudding and pie filling mix
⅓ cup sugar
1 packaged graham cracker crumb crust
  (6 ounces)
Reduced-calorie whipped topping

In a small saucepan sprinkle gelatin over water; let stand 3 minutes to soften. Stir over low heat until gelatin is completely dissolved. In food processor or blender combine gelatin mixture and remaining ingredients except crust and topping. Process until well blended. Pour into crust. Cover; chill several hours. Top with whipped topping.   *8 servings*

Nutritional information per serving:

250 Calories   6.5 g Fat   Less than 5 mg Cholesterol

Strawberry Brûlée

4 cups fresh strawberries, halved
½ cup soft-style or whipped cream cheese
½ cup DANNON® Vanilla Lowfat Yogurt
3 tablespoons packed brown sugar, divided

Arrange strawberries evenly in bottom of shallow 8-inch round broilerproof pan or 2-quart glass ceramic casserole. In a small bowl beat cream cheese, yogurt and 1 tablespoon brown sugar with electric mixer until smooth. Spoon yogurt mixture over fruit. Top with remaining 2 tablespoons brown sugar. Broil 4 to 5 inches from heat 2 to 3 minutes or just until brown sugar melts and starts to darken. Serve immediately.   *4 servings*

Nutritional information per serving:

200 Calories   11 g Fat   Less than 5 mg Cholesterol

Chocolate Silk Pie

Yogurt Drop Cookies

1¼ cups all-purpose flour
½ teaspoon baking soda
½ teaspoon grated orange peel
¼ cup shortening
¼ cup margarine or butter
⅔ cup sugar
1 egg
½ cup DANNON® Vanilla Lowfat Yogurt
1 teaspoon vanilla

Preheat oven to 350°F. Grease cookie sheets. In a medium bowl combine flour, baking soda and orange peel; set aside. In a large bowl beat shortening and margarine with electric mixer on medium speed for 30 seconds. Add sugar; beat on medium speed until fluffy. Beat in egg, yogurt and vanilla. Stir in flour mixture. Drop teaspoonfuls of dough, 2 inches apart, onto prepared cookie sheets. Bake 8 minutes or until golden brown. Remove to wire racks to cool.

36 cookies

Nutritional information per cookie:

60 Calories   3 g Fat   10 mg Cholesterol

Fruit Trifle

½ cup jellied cranberry sauce
3 tablespoons water
1 package (4-serving size) instant vanilla
   pudding mix
1 cup milk
1 cup DANNON® Vanilla or Lemon Lowfat
   Yogurt
1 package (3 ounces) ladyfingers (about 12),
   split
1½ cups fresh peach slices or frozen
   unsweetened peach slices, thawed, well
   drained and divided
1½ to 2 cups fresh strawberry halves, orange
   sections or grape halves, divided

In a small saucepan heat cranberry sauce and water until cranberry sauce is melted. Use wire whisk to beat until smooth. Cool. Prepare pudding mix according to package directions, using milk and yogurt in place of milk called for on package.

In a 1½-quart souffle dish or straight-sided serving bowl arrange enough of the ladyfingers to cover bottom and sides of dish. Combine 1 cup peaches and 1 cup strawberries. Spoon half of fruit mixture over ladyfingers in dish. Spread half of pudding mixture over fruit. Top with half of cranberry mixture. Arrange remaining ladyfingers on top. Repeat fruit and pudding layers. Spoon remaining cranberry mixture in center. Cover; chill at least 4 hours.

To serve, arrange remaining peaches and strawberries on top. Serve immediately. *8 servings*

Nutritional information per serving:

180 Calories   2 g Fat   45 mg Cholesterol

Lime Mousse Pie

1 package (4-serving size) lime gelatin
1 cup boiling water
1 cup marshmallow creme
1 cup DANNON® Plain Nonfat or Lowfat
   Yogurt
1 packaged graham cracker crumb crust
   (6 ounces)
   Sliced strawberries and kiwi fruit

Combine gelatin and boiling water in blender or with electric mixer. Blend on low speed 1 minute; blend on high speed 1 minute or until gelatin is completely dissolved. Add marshmallow creme; blend well on low speed. Add yogurt, blend on high speed. Pour into crust. Cover; chill several hours or overnight. Garnish with strawberries and kiwi fruit just before serving. *6 to 8 servings*

Nutritional information per serving:

360 Calories   8 g Fat   Less than 5 mg Cholesterol

Apple Cinnamon Tart

1½ cups quick-cooking oats
1 tablespoon plus ½ teaspoon ground cinnamon, divided
¾ cup frozen apple juice concentrate, thawed and divided
2 large apples, peeled, if desired and thinly sliced
1 teaspoon lemon juice
⅓ cup cold water
1 envelope unflavored gelatin
2 cups DANNON® Plain Nonfat or Lowfat Yogurt
¼ cup honey
½ teaspoon almond extract
Fresh mint leaves (optional)

Preheat oven to 350°F. In a small bowl combine oats and 1 tablespoon cinnamon. Toss with ¼ cup apple juice concentrate. Press onto bottom and side of 9-inch pie plate. Bake 5 minutes or until set. Cool on wire rack.

In a medium bowl toss apple slices with lemon juice; arrange on cooled crust in pan and set aside. In a small saucepan combine cold water and remaining ½ cup apple juice concentrate. Sprinkle gelatin over water mixture; let stand 3 minutes to soften. Cook and stir over medium heat until gelatin is completely dissolved; remove from heat. Add yogurt, honey, remaining ½ teaspoon cinnamon and almond extract; blend well. Pour over apples in crust. Chill several hours or overnight. If desired, garnish with mint leaves.   *10 servings*

Nutritional information per serving:

170 Calories   1.5 g Fat   Less than 5 mg Cholesterol

Apple Cinnamon Tart

Lemony Carrot Cake

1¼ cups all-purpose flour
½ teaspoon baking powder
½ teaspoon baking soda
½ teaspoon salt
⅓ cup margarine or butter
1 cup sugar
1 teaspoon grated lemon peel
1 teaspoon vanilla
2 eggs
½ cup DANNON® Plain, Lemon or Vanilla
      Lowfat Yogurt
1½ cups shredded carrots
      Lemon Yogurt Frosting (recipe follows)

Preheat oven to 350°F. Grease and lightly flour 9×9-inch baking pan. In a small bowl combine flour, baking powder, baking soda and salt. In a large bowl beat margarine with electric mixer 30 seconds. Add sugar, lemon peel and vanilla; beat well. Add eggs, 1 at a time, beating after each addition. Add flour mixture and yogurt alternately to margarine mixture, beating after each addition. Stir in carrots.

Pour batter into prepared pan; spread evenly. Bake 30 minutes or until toothpick inserted into center comes out clean. Cool in pan on wire rack. Spread cake with Lemon Yogurt Frosting. Garnish as desired.

9 servings

Lemon Yogurt Frosting

3 tablespoons margarine or butter
1½ cups sifted confectioner's sugar
½ teaspoon grated lemon peel
½ teaspoon vanilla
1 to 2 tablespoons DANNON® Plain, Lemon
      or Vanilla Lowfat Yogurt

In a small bowl beat margarine until softened. Gradually add confectioner's sugar; beat well. Beat in lemon peel and vanilla. Add enough yogurt to make a spreadable frosting.

Nutritional information per serving:

350 Calories   13 g Fat   60 mg Cholesterol

Lemony Carrot Cake

Ginger Cake with Yogurt-Rum Sauce

2 cups all-purpose flour
2 teaspoons ground cinnamon
1¾ teaspoons ground ginger
1½ teaspoons ground nutmeg
¾ teaspoon baking powder
¾ teaspoon baking soda
½ teaspoon ground cloves
⅛ teaspoon salt
¾ cup molasses
2 eggs
6 tablespoons light olive oil or vegetable oil
¼ cup sugar
½ cup DANNON® Vanilla Lowfat Yogurt
½ cup boiling water
Yogurt-Rum Sauce (recipe follows)

Preheat oven to 350°F. Spray 8×8-inch baking pan with vegetable cooking spray. In a large bowl combine flour, cinnamon, ginger, nutmeg, baking powder, baking soda, cloves and salt; set aside.

In a medium bowl whisk together molasses, eggs, oil and sugar until well blended. Whisk in yogurt, then boiling water. Pour half the molasses mixture into dry ingredients; stir just until dry ingredients are moistened. Add remaining molasses mixture; stir just until blended. (Batter will be slightly lumpy.) Pour batter into prepared pan.

Bake 45 to 55 minutes or until toothpick inserted into center comes out clean. (Cake surface will crack.) Cool on wire rack at least 30 minutes before serving. Flavor will improve with standing. Serve with Yogurt-Rum Sauce.   *12 servings*

Yogurt-Rum Sauce

½ cup DANNON® Vanilla Lowfat Yogurt
4 teaspoons confectioner's sugar
¾ teaspoon dark rum

In a small serving bowl combine yogurt, confectioner's sugar and rum; stir well.

Nutritional information per serving:
280 Calories   8 g Fat   45 mg Cholesterol

Easy Fruit Shortcake

1½ cups packaged *complete* pancake mix
3 tablespoons packed brown sugar
¼ cup shortening
1 egg, beaten
2 cups DANNON® Plain, Lemon or Vanilla
    Lowfat Yogurt, divided
1 package (8 ounces) cream cheese, softened
¼ cup sifted confectioner's sugar
2 cups assorted fresh fruit (sliced
    strawberries, sliced bananas, sliced
    peaches, blueberries and raspberries)

Preheat oven to 350°F. Grease 8-inch round baking pan. In a large bowl combine pancake mix and brown sugar. Cut in shortening with pastry blender or 2 knives until mixture resembles coarse crumbs.

In a small bowl combine egg and 1 cup yogurt. Add egg mixture all at once to dry ingredients; stir just until moistened.

Spread dough in prepared pan. Bake 15 minutes or until set (*do not overbake*). Cool in pan 10 minutes; remove from pan. Cool completely on wire rack. In a small bowl beat cream cheese and confectioner's sugar until creamy. Stir in remaining 1 cup yogurt.

To assemble shortcake, carefully cut cake horizontally into 2 layers. Place bottom layer on serving plate. Spoon half the cream cheese mixture onto bottom layer; top with half of fruit. Place remaining shortcake layer, cut side down, on top of fruit layer. Spread top with remaining cream cheese mixture. Arrange remaining fruit on top. Serve immediately. *6 servings*

Nutritional information per serving:

370 Calories   17 g Fat   70 mg Cholesterol

No-Guilt Cheesecake

4 cups DANNON® Plain Lowfat or Nonfat
   Yogurt
½ cup graham cracker crumbs
1 tablespoon margarine or butter, melted
1 cup lowfat cottage cheese
3 egg whites
¾ cup sugar
2 tablespoons all-purpose flour
1 tablespoon fresh lemon juice
1 teaspoon vanilla
   Sliced fresh fruit
   Fresh mint leaves (optional)

Spoon yogurt into large strainer lined with double thickness of cheesecloth or a coffee filter. Place bowl beneath, but not touching strainer to catch liquid. Chill 24 hours. Discard liquid.

Preheat oven to 325°F. In a small bowl combine crumbs and melted margarine. Press evenly into bottom of 7- to 9-inch springform pan; set aside. In food processor or blender combine cottage cheese and egg whites. Process until smooth, scraping down side of container occasionally. Add drained yogurt, sugar, flour, lemon juice and vanilla. Process an additional 30 seconds or until well blended, scraping down side of container occasionally. Pour into crust. Place pan on baking sheet.

Bake 1 hour or until set. Cool to room temperature. Cover; chill several hours or overnight. Serve with fruit. If desired, garnish with mint leaves.   *12 servings*

Nutritional information per serving:
140 Calories   2.5 g Fat   5 mg Cholesterol

No-Guilt Cheesecake

Orange-Filled Cream Puffs

¾ cup granulated sugar
3 tablespoons cornstarch
1½ cups orange juice
3 egg yolks, beaten
1 cup DANNON® Plain or Vanilla Lowfat
    Yogurt
2 tablespoons margarine or butter
6 Cream Puffs (recipe follows)
1 can (11 ounces) mandarin orange sections,
    drained
Confectioner's sugar

In a medium saucepan combine granulated sugar, cornstarch and orange juice. Cook and stir over medium heat until bubbly; cook and stir 2 minutes more. Remove from heat. Gradually stir half of hot mixture into egg yolks. Return to saucepan. Bring to a boil. Reduce heat. Cook and stir 2 minutes more. Remove from heat. Stir in yogurt and margarine. Cover; chill 4 hours.

To serve, spoon filling into bottoms of cream puffs. Pile orange sections on top of filling. Add cream puff tops. Lightly sift confectioner's sugar over tops. *6 servings*

Cream Puffs: Preheat oven to 400°F. Grease baking sheet. In a medium saucepan combine 1 cup water and ½ cup margarine. Bring to a boil, stirring until margarine melts. Add 1 cup all-purpose flour and ½ teaspoon salt all at once, stirring vigorously. Cook and stir until mixture forms a ball that does not separate. Remove from heat and cool 10 minutes. Add 4 eggs, 1 at a time, beating after each addition until mixture is smooth.

Drop heaping tablespoons of batter into 10 mounds, 3 inches apart, onto prepared baking sheet. Bake about 35 minutes or until golden brown and puffy. Cool slightly. Cut off tops and remove any soft dough inside. Cool completely on wire rack. Freeze remaining cream puffs for later use. *10 cream puffs*

Nutritional information per serving:

310 Calories   16 g Fat   195 mg Cholesterol

Orange-Filled Cream Puffs

Chocolate Fruit Torte

½ cup margarine or butter
3 tablespoons unsweetened cocoa
¼ cup water
1 cup all-purpose flour
1 cup sugar
½ teaspoon baking soda
¼ teaspoon salt
1 egg, slightly beaten
1 cup DANNON® Vanilla or Lemon Lowfat
Yogurt, divided
1 teaspoon vanilla
½ cup whipping cream
1 can (11 ounces) mandarin orange sections,
drained
2 kiwi fruit, peeled and sliced
3 or 4 strawberries, sliced
1 slice carambola (star fruit) (optional)

Preheat oven to 350°F. Grease and lightly flour 9-inch round baking pan. In a medium saucepan combine margarine, cocoa and water. Bring to a boil, stirring constantly. Remove from heat.

In a large bowl combine flour, sugar, baking soda and salt. Stir in egg, ¼ cup yogurt and vanilla. Blend in cocoa mixture. Pour batter into prepared pan. Bake 40 minutes or until set. Cool in pan 10 minutes. Remove from pan; cool on wire rack.

Just before serving, prepare filling. In a large bowl beat whipping cream with electric mixer on high speed until soft peaks form. Gently fold in remaining ¾ cup yogurt. Carefully cut cake horizontally into 2 layers. Place bottom layer on serving plate. Spread half of filling on bottom half. Top with mandarin orange sections, reserving 6 sections for garnish. Top with remaining cake layer, cut side down. Spread remaining filling on top. Arrange reserved orange sections, kiwi fruit slices, strawberry slices and carambola slice on top.   *10 servings*

Nutritional information per serving:
290 Calories   15 g Fat   45 mg Cholesterol

Chocolate Fruit Torte

Creamy Citrus Cheesecake

¾ cup graham cracker crumbs
2 tablespoons margarine or butter, melted
3 eggs
½ cup granulated sugar
1 teaspoon grated orange peel
¼ cup orange juice
3 teaspoons vanilla, divided
2 packages (8 ounces *each*) cream cheese
1 cup DANNON® Plain, Lemon or Vanilla
    Lowfat Yogurt, divided
2 tablespoons confectioners' sugar
Fresh fruit (optional)

Preheat oven to 325°F. In a medium bowl combine crumbs and melted margarine. Press onto bottom of 7-inch springform pan. Bake 6 minutes or until set. Cool on wire rack.

In food processor or blender combine eggs, granulated sugar, orange peel, orange juice and 2 teaspoons vanilla. Cut cream cheese into chunks; add to food processor and process until smooth. Stir in ½ cup yogurt. Pour into crust. Place on baking sheet. Bake 50 to 60 minutes or until almost set.

In a small bowl combine remaining ½ cup yogurt, confectioners' sugar and remaining 1 teaspoon vanilla. Spread over hot cheesecake. Loosen side of pan. Cool on wire rack; chill. To serve, carefully remove side of pan. If desired, garnish with fruit.   *8 servings*

Nutritional information per serving:

360 Calories   26 g Fat   170 mg Cholesterol

INDEX

METRIC CONVERSION CHART

VOLUME MEASUREMENT (dry)

⅛ teaspoon = .5 mL
¼ teaspoon = 1 mL
½ teaspoon = 2 mL
¾ teaspoon = 4 mL
1 teaspoon = 5 mL
1 tablespoon = 15 mL
2 tablespoons = 25 mL
¼ cup = 50 mL
⅓ cup = 75 mL
⅔ cup = 150 mL
¾ cup = 175 mL
1 cup = 250 mL
2 cups = 1 pint = 500 mL
3 cups = 750 mL
4 cups = 1 quart = 1 L

VOLUME MEASUREMENT (fluid)

1 fluid ounce (2 tablespoons) = 30 mL
4 fluid ounces (½ cup) = 125 mL
8 fluid ounces (1 cup) = 250 mL
12 fluid ounces (1½ cups) = 375 mL
16 fluid ounces (2 cups) = 500 mL

WEIGHT (MASS)

½ ounce = 15 g
1 ounce = 30 g
3 ounces = 85 g
3.75 ounces = 100 g
4 ounces = 115 g
8 ounces = 225 g
12 ounces = 340 g
16 ounces = 1 pound = 450 g

DIMENSION

1/16 inch = 2 mm
⅛ inch = 3 mm
¼ inch = 6 mm
½ inch = 1.5 cm
¾ inch = 2 cm
1 inch = 2.5 cm

OVEN TEMPERATURES

250°F = 120°C
275°F = 140°C
300°F = 150°C
325°F = 160°C
350°F = 180°C
375°F = 190°C
400°F = 200°C
425°F = 220°C
450°F = 230°C

BAKING PAN SIZES

Utensil	Inches/ Quarts	Metric Volume	Centimeters
Baking or	8×8×2	2 L	20×20 ×5
Cake pan	9×9×2	2.5 L	22×22 ×5
(square or	12×8×2	3 L	30×20 ×5
rectangular)	13×9×2	3.5 L	33×23 ×5
Loaf Pan	8×4×3	1.5 L	20×10 ×7
	9×5×3	2 L	23×13 ×7
Round Layer	8×1½	1.2 L	20×4
Cake Pan	9×1½	1.5 L	23×4
Pie Plate	8×1¼	750 mL	20×3
	9×1¼	1 L	23×3
Baking Dish	1 quart	1 L	
or	1½ quart	1.5 L	
Casserole	2 quart	2 L	